Barbie™ Exclusives

IDENTIFICATION
&
VALUES

FEATURING:
DEPARTMENT STORE SPECIALS
PORCELAIN TREASURES
& DISNEY

Cover design Beth Summers
Book design Joyce Cherry

Searching For A Publisher?

We are always looking for knowledgeable people considered to be experts within their fields. If you feel that there is a real need for a book on your collectible subject and have a large comprehensive collection contact Collector Books.

Printed by IMAGE GRAPHICS, INC., Paducah, Kentucky

Acknowledgments

The place to start is with anyone who ever gave me, sold me, or bought from me a Barbie doll. All of these elements have given me the opportunity to compile this collection so that I can share it with you. Those who helped me in other ways include:

Helen Vuckovich, who informed me that Kodak Brownie is passé, and that there were better cameras on the market today.

Russ' Camera, who sold me my equipment, and who didn't laugh at me when I told them I didn't know what an f-stop was.

Debby Shapiro, for telling me to go to Russ' and for driving up and down the state securing dolls for me, making sure I didn't miss anything.

Carolyn Klemovec for her patience and guidance in helping me comb, clean, and primp, not only the dolls you see here, but all those in my private collection.

Patti Guttshall for helping me at the store, helping me put together a fine display at the public library, and encouraging me to get on with this book.

Bob Gardner for lending me a doll I couldn't get my hands on and for sharing additional information I was not aware of.

Sarah Eames for not wanting to do this book.

Mr. Styers for encouraging me.

Aunt Katy who bought me my first Barbie back in 1959.

Mom and Dad, for supporting me in everything, especially my mid-life crises career change.

Most importantly, my husband Gary (a.k.a. Mr. Margo) for recognizing that Barbie is more than a nostalgic journey to me, for recognizing great investment potential, for not giving me too much of a hard time when I spend too much (how can you spend too much?), for encouraging me to buy my first #1 when they were only $500.00, and for driving me up and down the state of California to doll shows.

Introduction

Many changes started to occur at Mattel in the 1980's. Executives recognized the potential for additional sales by targeting collectors in addition to children. Inspired by additional revenue, they created "The Timeless Creation" division. The Dolls of the World Collection, commonly referred to as the "International," was Mattel's strongest category for the advanced collectors. These dolls were originally only sold in "better" department stores. From this came the expression, "department store special." Mattel is now referring to any doll done exclusively for any given company as "customized" Barbie dolls. You will be hearing this terminology more and more as time passes; but for the purpose of this book I will refer to this "customized" category as exclusive, for this is how we presently refer to them.

In a manner of a few short years, Mattel recognized collector interest and a need to expand their thinking and product line. This expansion would not only increase sales and stockholder happiness, but also create a need for labor across the globe.

A new sales division and a design department were established to cultivate new clients for its unprecedented campaign to market specialty dolls. The sales department would target potential buyers for special limited edition dolls. The design department would create dolls and fashions for specific companies. The sales department would present what the design department had put together to the store buyers. The promise that this doll and design would be done especially for them and not be sold in any other establishment gave the product enormous prestige. The opportunity to have an exclusive was attractive to many companies and the smart ones took the bait.

Mattel had been producing exclusives for companies since the early 1960's. The best known is Sears. This new expansion has generated new terminology and a new challenge for the collector because now most of the companies offering exclusives are not better department stores, the term "department store special" has been dropped from our vocabulary, and the expression "E x c l u s i v e" took its place.

My book is set up alphabetically and then sub sorted by the patent date on the box. The year on the box in some situations may not be the date the doll was released into the market place. I have chosen to utilize the box date so that there is consistency and less confusion.

The challenge for collectors is acquiring these harder-to-find dolls. Many stores who participate in the exclusive program are not found in all parts of the country. This makes it difficult for collectors to acquire these Barbie dolls for their collection. Collectors are happy to turn to smaller dealers and shopkeepers who are willing to work for them and help them get those harder-to-find Barbie dolls.

A word about the price guide: many collectors get frustrated with price guides. There really isn't any reason to upset yourself over this. The term "guide" is just that, a guide, not a hard and fast rule. Product availability is territorial. Economics 101, supply and demand is the greater factor. Only you can determine if that Barbie is worth the price you are being asked, and even if it seems high to you today think about tomorrow's potential. Most importantly, buy what you like, whatever the value or price.

Many of you may be disappointed that Toys Я Us is not represented. There are two good reasons for the omission. First, this book is already crowded with pictures of exclusives. I wanted to give you a complete look at the truly harder-to-find dolls. All the vivid close-ups enable collectors and dealers alike to identify played-with dolls more easily. Second, there are enough Toys Я Us Barbie exclusives to fill a whole new book, so I have an excuse to write another book and you have something to look forward to.

Contents

Party in Pink • 1991 • $35.00

This leggings-and-lace outfit, done specifically for Ames, reflects Barbie doll's ability to change her wardrobe as fashions change with the times. This is what young people were wearing to school in 1991. This outfit appeared in the 1992 Mattel catalog as a Magic Teen Talk fashion that was never delivered.

Hot Looks • 1991 • $30.00

Hot pink and royal blue is not a color combination we see very often. These primaries look terrific on this Hot Looks Barbie.

Denim 'n Lace • 1992 • $35.00

Much thought and careful workmanship went into Barbie doll's
outfit. You really get a lot for
your money with her.

Country Looks • 1992 • $25.00

Western influenced attire has always been a good seller for Mattel. So when Ames selected this theme for their fourth exclusive, they automatically had a winner on their hands.

Barbie Style • 1990 • $45.00

We were under the impression that Applause originally intended to have a series of dolls in plastic and figurines in porcelain, as well as mugs and miniatures. Two years after their first exclusive, Barbie Style, was released, Applause quit producing. Applause then reduced the price of leftover dolls to rock bottom prices and resale values plummeted temporarily.

Holiday Doll • 1991 • $45.00

Applause Barbie was made with elegant fabric and excellent workmanship. Both Applause dolls' boxes were simple and sturdy, with removable lids that allow collectors to display their dolls without removing them from the box. I'm surprised Mattel doesn't use this shoe-box style more often.

Feelin' Groovy • 1986 • $175.00

BillyBoy is a designer of adult cloth-ing. He and Mattel struck up a deal which resulted in two BillyBoy Bar-bie dolls and a national tour, an unprecedented event for Barbie. Feelin' Groovy was the first "designer doll" Mattel had. She was sold only in better department stores. This doll has always been extremely popular with collectors.

Nouveau Théâtre de la Mode • $250.00

BillyBoy's second doll can be found in two versions: with black fingernail polish (as you see here) or without. BillyBoy was able to convince top designers from around the world to put their expertise to work making fashions for Barbie. The dolls were dressed, sets were designed, and BillyBoy arranged a road tour so that people all over the U. S. had an opportunity to see top couture fashions on display. Note the tour poster behind Barbie.

Dance Club Gift Set • 1989 • $75.00

Children's Palace had three dolls before it closed its doors. Dance Club Barbie came with a doll and tape player. It is a cute concept. Mattel had hoped the Dance Club group would be as popular as the Rockers had been.

≈ ❦ ≈

Barbie • 1990 • $45.00

All Mattel has to do is put Mouseketeer ears on a doll and she sells like hot cakes. Not that this cute doll wouldn't have sold on her own, but I'm sure those ears contributed to sales. She received no fancy name, was just known as Barbie.

≈ ❦ ≈

Barbie • 1990 • $45.00

Children's Palace black Barbie with the Christie face mold had the exact same outfit as the white version. Each came with an extra pair of long pants with a gold ruffle down the side.

Disney Fun Barbie • 1992 • $45.00

Disney and Mattel are truly a win-win combination. Disney Fun, an exclusive for Disneyland and Disney World was a sure seller. Note that her special fabric is designed just for Barbie with Mickey Mouse silhouettes. The Mickey Mouse balloon she carries is hard plastic, just like the one the Heart family had when they went to Disneyland in the late 1980's.

Pirates of the Caribbean • 1993 • $35.00

Mattel and Disney decided on the first rooted-beard doll based on one of Disneyland's most popular attractions, Pirates of the Caribbean. His elaborate face paint emphasizes his hard character, making him particularly interesting to little boys who like to play hard.

~ ❧ ~

Mary Poppins • 1993 • $35.00

Is there anyone who hasn't seen Julie Andrews star in Disney's feature film *Mary Poppins*? Mary's popularity is enhanced by the fantasy that someone will take care of us the way we take care of our dolls.

~ ❧ ~

Davy Crockett • 1993 • $45.00

The ever-popular Davy Crockett is hard to find. I'm not sure if it's Davy's popularity with collectors, his popularity with little boys, or a low production level that keeps him off the shelves. I'm happy he's part of my collection.

Peter Pan • 1993 • $35.00

I was probably five when I first saw *Peter Pan*. I was dropped off at the theater in Southampton, New York and found myself in fantasyland for weeks thereafter. I was hoping for the same emotional sensation from this three doll series. Their ability to fly is unique.

Tinker Bell • 1993 • $35.00

Those of us who collect old Barbie dolls, and Liddle Kid- dles, may have expected to see Tinker Bell in miniature. I was disappointed to see the Skip- per face mold. However I do love her outfit, especially those wings.

Wendy • 1993 • $35.00

Here we have another Skipper dressed as Wendy. Can you tell I'm disappointed? As a collector, I say "Make a new face mold and just charge me for it." If I were a mother buying a toy for my child I'd probably say "I'm not paying extra for that." And yet, there isn't a mother out there who doesn't remember how important these little things were to her as a child.

Toontown Stacie • 1993 • $35.00

Disney's newest release at the time of publication is this cute little Stacie going to meet Disney Fun Barbie at the park. Stacy wears a special Toontown T-shirt and carries a Mickey Mouse balloon.

Gay Parisienne • 1991 • $750.00

In 1991 Disney World put on a spectacular show which included a special event referred to as the "Showcase of Dolls." Mattel was asked to participate in this event. They agreed to make a special limited edition of blonde Gay Parisienne porcelains. This was identical to the Timeless Creation division brunette. The blonde was to be limited to only 300 pieces. And then...

Gay Parisienne • 1991 • $750.00

All collectors of vintage Barbie dolls know that this #1 reproduction face was never made as a redhead. So why is she here? When Disney World decided to sponsor their showcase of dolls, they reached an agreement with Mattel to do the limited edition Gay Parisienne blonde. By mistake, some of the blondes were shipped to other companies. Some of these dolls were then sold to the general public. Mattel, despite good intentions of righting the situation, could not retrieve all the blondes. Because this was to have been a Disney World exclusive, what could be done? Mattel generously and quickly created this wonderful redhead. She was limited to 300 pieces, making collectors extremely happy. These two, combined with the regular Gay Parisienne porcelain, are referred to as the trilogy. An odd number of dolls makes for better display. Carol Spencer was the designer of this terrific doll.

Trilogy Gay Parisienne

Plantation Belle • 1992 • $750.00

There were no hard feelings and Mattel was invited to again participate in Disney World's "Showcase of Dolls." Plantation Belle was originally done as a redhead for Mattel's better accounts and specialty doll stores. She was limited to Disney World as a blonde. Her production level was only 300 pieces. The designer for this doll was Karen Victor, who also gave us our 35th Nostalgic Gift Set.

Crystal Rhapsody • 1992 • $750.00

In 1993 we got to see our first and only Disneyland porcelain. This year Mattel and Disney decided on Crystal Rhapsody Barbie. The original Crystal Rhapsody was a blonde and was available only through the mail-order division of Mattel. Crystal had the lowest production level of all the exclusive porcelains at 250 pieces. Cynthia Young was the designer for Crystal Rhapsody, and was at the park to sign dolls. Please remember that the date refers to patent date not necessarily the year the dolls were released.

Silken Flame • 1993 • $750.00

Silken Flame Barbie as a brunette was designed by Carol Spencer of Mattel. Mattel participated in what Disney was now billing as "Walt Disney's Teddy Bear and Doll Convention." For their special doll, Mattel chose Silken Flame Barbie as a blonde, only 400 pieces. Carol Spencer was invited to be on hand to sign the porcelains. You could have your picture taken with Ms. Spencer as she autographed your doll.

Collectors often like to have their dolls signed by the person who originally designed the doll. Here we see Carol Spencer, long time designer at Mattel, in Disney World's Tinker Bell store ready to autograph Silken Flame Barbie.

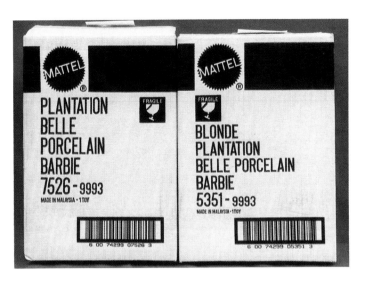

⊸ ⸎ ⊸

Shipping cartons can be useful for protecting real boxes. They are shown here to point out that after the Gay Parisienne mistake, Mattel either changed stock number, noted hair color, or did both to prevent future mix-ups.

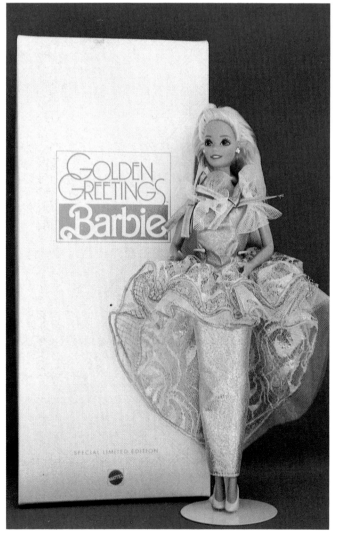

Golden Greetings • 1989 • $250.00

FAO Schwarz, a prestigious toy store catering to an affluent clientele, bought their first exclusive Barbie in 1989. Released around the holidays, she was appropriately named Golden Greetings. There is a general rule of thumb that the first doll of any series is the most valuable. But on the next page you will find the second FAO doll that continues to take that honor away from Golden Greetings.

Winter Fantasy • 1990 • $250.00

This second FAO exclusive is extremely popular. Velvet garbed dolls with faux fur trim are among collectors' favorites. Note that my doll has no earrings. She originally came with blue plastic button earrings, which I took out. Mattel didn't realize that the blue dye in the earring would cause the plastic around Barbie doll's ears to turn blue. I was fortunate that the acne cream treatments removed the dye from my doll. Luckily, the problem was identified early. Mattel had not shut down production and was able to manufacture new head replacements which had silver earrings substituted.

Night Sensation • 1991 • $150.00

With the increased demand for FAO exclusives, production level was increased on Night Sensation, their third doll. This allowed more collectors to acquire her and also depressed her value somewhat.

Madison Avenue • 1991 • $175.00

Mattel came up with a shopping theme for themselves. It included such dolls as City Style, Meijer's, and Madison Avenue Barbie. (Shown here). The production level was high and the demand for her was stronger than for Night Sensation. The strong demand helped her value to escalate. Cute, isn't she?

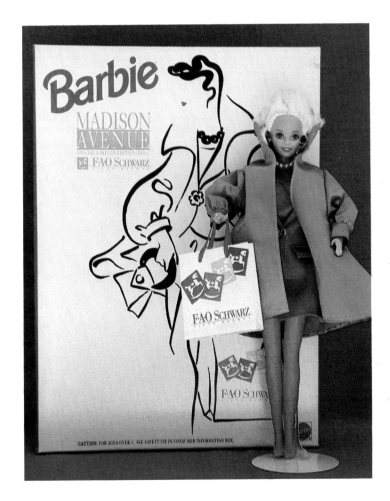

Rockette • 1992 • $175.00

1992 marked the 60th anniversary of Radio City Music Hall. What better theme for a New York based firm like FAO Schwarz? Isn't it interesting that this doll has not been coined as a gift set? But she is: you get not only another costume for Barbie, but a paper doll as well. She could be considered the fore-runner to the Hollywood celebrity series. She is the kick-off to the theater and movie concept. I predict this grouping will prove to be a raving success. (Note that Barbie doll's bodysuit is the same fabric used on Sweet Lavender from Woolworth's, pg.153.)

Silver Screen • 1993 • $175.00

Another gift set for FAO, Silver Screen, has all the glamour and sophistication of Marilyn Monroe, and yet hair style, make-up, and gown are timeless. This unique combination will allow all ages to relate to their favorite celebrity, be it Tallulah, Marilyn, or Madonna. Ann Driskill designed both the box and the doll. This is the first exclusive whose box bears the name of the Mattel designer.

Party Lace • 1989 • $45.00

Even with a few hairs out of place, wouldn't you like your hair to look like this in the morning? Barbie is simply constructed and originally inexpensively priced just for Hills. This allows collectors on limited budgets an opportunity to own exclusives. She sold well enough that Hills was able to select a more elaborately constructed doll the next year.

Evening Sparkle • 1990 • $40.00

Second for Hills is Evening Sparkle. Hills was smart to recognize the interest for fancier dolls. I don't see this doll very much at shows and yet she is not classified as hard to find. Actually, because the Hills stores are not located in California I rarely see any of their dolls here.

Moonlight Rose • 1991 • $35.00

I can't think of any other Barbie wearing raspberry, can you? As a brunette, I fancy these jewel tones. It was the color of Moonlight Rose's gown that first attracted me to her. However, she just isn't that popular. Maybe it's because her skirt was bulky, or maybe it was because she should have been a brunette. (I bet the designers at Mattel just love it when we chatter on about what we would have done, as if we could do a better job. If I really could, I'd be working at Mattel.)

Blue Elegance • 1992 • $35.00

Three out of four of the Hill dolls are wearing primary colors. It's a nice change from pastels. Every time I look at Blue Elegance, I envision the NBC Peacock. I am fond of this gown.

Evening Flame • 1991 • $125.00

Evening Flame Barbie was the first for Home Shopping Club. She is a limited edition and comes complete with paper to prove it. I left Evening Flame in her box so you can see how the liner makes her look pale. Compare this with the close-up. Doesn't she look like a completely different doll? Backgrounds can make or break a doll. Check your Black Extravaganza. My first impression of her was weak, yet she is gorgeous once she was removed from the box. Both these dolls improve dramatically when not set against their original background. Evening Flame Barbie was the first exclusive to come with a numbered certificate; two more were to follow.

Winter Princess • 1993 • $600.00

This was to have been an exclusive for Home Shopping. Speciality doll shops across the nation were thrilled when Mattel decided to share Winter Princess with them. This doll must have set a record as the fastest appreciating Barbie of all times. I attribute it to the velvet and fur trim combination. Note how her eye shadow is enhanced by the matching colors used on the background of her liner. The artwork on her box allows the imagination to take over and create our own love story.

Evergreen Princess • 1994 • $125.00

Evergreen Princess is the follow-up doll to Winter Princess. Based on early orders, all indications are that she is *hot*.

Peach Pretty • 1989 • $45.00

Sometimes you buy a doll NRFB and you just don't know what she went through before she was put in that box. I seldom buy a doll and leave her in the box for more than ten minutes. But for no particular reason I let Peach Pretty stay in her box until I took this picture. I've had her for years and never noticed her nose nip. So, no it's not the photo. But she's been with me a long time and I like her anyway.

Pretty in Purple • 1992 • $45.00

K-Mart does a roaring business, so I'm surprised that to date they have only these three exclusives. Even at that, several years passed before K-Mart offered us Pretty in Purple. When I look at her, I always think of Woolworth's Sweet Lavender. Having been produced the same year, they display well together.

Pretty in Purple • 1992 • $45.00

The Christie face mold was used here. Her dress and accessories are the same as those used with the white version. Barbie doll's eye make-up, however, is very different. Here you see much more eye shadow.

Wacky Warehouse I • 1992 • $65.00

Kool-Aid's Wacky Warehouse I promotional is bright and cheerful. Barbie is ready for town and beach. We don't see many dolls with braids; the only other one I can think of is the Mackie bride. To acquire this special item you had to drink a lot of Kool-Aid, save up package points, and mail them in to get your premium doll. (This doll was released in 1993).

Wacky Warehouse II • 1994 • $65.00

This premium Barbie required the same thirstiness as the first Kool–Aid doll. Saving up those points can float you. This Wacky Warehouse doll had a box change. An extra bonus with this doll is a special 35th anniversary certificate. She is enclosed in a sealed shoe box, a more sophisticated packaging. This doll, like the first one, is ready for a day at the beach.

Treasures • 1994 • $65.00

Kraft Foods, the same company that brings us Kool-Aid, now has a "customized" Barbie. To get her, you had to eat as much macaroni and cheese as you had to drink Kool-Aid. After opening the boxes, emptying the contents, and clipping out the mandatory number of points, you could send in for your doll. This Barbie doll's outfit and box have color accents that are the color of American cheese. The Kraft logo is on her shirt, hat, and bag. She's a happy doll.

Little Debbie • 1992 • $75.00

Kool-Aid, Little Debbie Snacks, and Kraft are all great products, but how much can you ingest to acquire enough points to get their dolls? If Hershey had one I'd be ordering them by the dozens in no time flat! I'd also be the size of a barn. Little Debbie isn't Barbie, she's Little Debbie. I have her on display in the Magical Mansion in the kitchen, baking a cake for Skipper's 30th birthday party. The only way you could get the Little Debbie doll was to find a snack box that included the order form printed on the back of the box. There weren't enough dolls to go around and several orders were not filled. She's the only one to date done for Little Debbie Snacks.

Barbie • 1991 • N/A

This doll is on loan from Bob Gardner. I was surprised to discover there was another customized doll out there. Bob was kind enough to not only lend her to me, but let me take her out of the box too. All I know is that Barbie was made for a cake company that does a lot of decorating. Mc Glynn's also had a black version wearing a blue dress. She is impossible to find, so no sense looking . Thanks Bob, for sharing.

Something Extra • 1992 • $35.00

In 1992, Meijers (pronounced my–ers), joined the exclusive program with a simple straight-haired, straight-armed doll. She wears a simple, seldom seen Swiss dot fabric. Barbie came with a book of discount Barbie coupons which were redeemable at Meijers stores only.

~ ~❦~ ~

Shopping Fun • 1992 • $30.00

Meijers second doll, Shopping Fun Barbie, is truly ready to shop. She has her shopping bag and comes complete with her own child-size checkbook. The checks enclosed were really store coupons, again redeemable only at Meijers. For little girls who bought the doll, this was probably their first experience with a checkbook. You got a lot with this doll. You could even send away for a genuine Barbie buck. It is legal tender, so if you got desperate you could spend it.

~ ~❦~ ~

Picnic Pretty • 1992 • $25.00

This is the one and only exclusive doll that Osco has had to date. Barbie is ready for a casual day of picnicking. We don't see gingham very often, but in 1992 we got two gingham girls; the other was Little Debbie.

Evening Elegance • 1990 • $65.00

Plain wrap boxes, as seen here on JC Penney's first exclusive Evening Elegance, have been used historically by Mattel for mail-order companies (like Sears and Wards in the 1960's). They are not visually attractive to the collector, but do cut costs to the consumer and are of interest to the Barbie historian. There are two different dress versions. Since the mail-order store Barbie dolls came in sealed boxes, customers didn't know what they were getting until they opened them. I'm sorry I don't have the other dress to show you.

Enchanted Evening • 1991 • $95.00

One of my very favorites is this JC
Penney Barbie, Enchanted Evening.
Sometimes I display her with other
fur trimmed dolls, but right now
she's next to Feeling Groovy. The fabric of her coat is the same as we saw
on an M. C. Hammer fashion. JC
Penney had received so many com-
plaints on the Evening Elegance
packaging that Enchanted Evening
was put in a window box.

Evening Sensation • 1992 • $55.00

I initially had trouble with this doll. I thought her attire was more matronly than a glamour Barbie doll should be and her hair was uncooperative when I took her out of the box. But since my friend Carolyn fixed her, Evening Sensation has grown on me and I appreciate the doll more.

Golden Winter • 1993 • $55.00

Golden Winter Barbie expresses warmth and sophistication. They selected wonderful fabric for this doll. We don't see many black-grounded prints for Barbie. This paisley has just enough color to perk her up and still maintain elegance. One of the things not evident in the photos is that all the Penney's dolls have metallic shoes which are only produced by Estrela Company. Estrela is Mattel's licensee company in Brazil. It wasn't until JC Penney that any of these shoes were used by Mattel Incorporated, USA.

Earring Magic Barbie • 1991 • $125.00

It was a surprise to find an exclusive at Radio Shack. This Earring Magic Barbie, complete with a computer software pak, is not well known. The cost of her software quickly put her out of reach for many Barbie collectors.

Celebration • 1985 • $95.00

1986 marked Sears 100th anniversary. Promotional advertising for Sears' birthday was started a year in advance, it included this special edition Celebration Barbie. She comes with a special silver wrist tag to commemorate the event. This was not the first exclusive Sears had, by any means, but it is the first I cover in this time frame.

Star Dream • 1987 • $80.00

Celebration was released in 1986; the following year Sears added a second doll to the collection. The plastic trim used on her headband and waist may look familiar to you. It was used on the Brazilian doll from the Dolls of the World series. It's not often that fabrics repeat on other dolls. Mattel either got a great buy on the fabric, or they bought too much and were able to find good use for it. Star Dream had a sister doll named Skating Star/Étoile du Patin. She was made by Mattel Toronto as an official souvenir doll of the 1988 Calgary Winter Olympics and carries the official Olympic seal.

STARDREAM™
Barbie Doll
Evening sparkle..
long and short!

Lilac & Lovely • 1987 • $70.00

Lilac, lavender, and purple are colors that collectors are attracted to. Because of the wording on her box, she is sometimes referred to as Lilac and Lace, causing confusion. Lilac & Lovely, Lavender Surprise, and Walmart's Lavender Looks are easily mixed up.

Evening Enchantment • 1989 • $60.00

Evening Enchantment was the first in the series to have her hair pulled back off her face, allowing us to see how nicely her eyes are painted. Her gown is a bit less elaborate than those on the other Sears dolls.

Lavender Surprise • 1989 • $50.00

Lavender Surprise has a gown that is very versatile in design. It can be long or short. However, it must be tough to walk when the skirt is long; it's tight at her ankles. This is the first and only black doll in the series. Compare the close-ups and note how different their eyes are painted.

Southern Belle • 1991 • $40.00

Plantation themes, the Old South, are always popular concepts with collectors. It denotes demure femininity, a time of grace and manners. When ordering this doll by mail, be sure to specify that you want Sears Southern Belle because there is also a Victorian Southern Belle from the Great Era's collection.

Dream Princess • 1992 • $40.00

Dream Princess lives in the shadow of Blossom Beautiful. Sears had two dolls in 1993. In a panic to acquire Blossom Beautiful, many collectors forgot to buy Dream Princess. She costs considerably less money and is well worth more then list price.

Blossom Beautiful • 1992 • $400.00

Blossom Beautiful was released at the same time that Sears made the economic decision to close down their mail-order department. She was not sold in the store. Sears' shipping department got a little sloppy and when it came time to ship the orders on file, they shoved the dolls in a plastic bag with no protection and sent them to their customers. When collectors saw crushed boxes, many returned them. Production had been cut short and many never received replacements. Blossom Beautiful is rare. Many collectors have all the other Sears dolls and want the complete collection, causing demand to be high for a very limited doll.

Enchanted Princess • 1993 • $75.00

Sears in Canada obtained a doll named Enchanted Princess, making Americans jealous. Her opening price was very reasonable, but after shipping and customs charges, her price jumped. She was originally designed for Sears here in the United States. Unfortunately for us, when Sears dissolved their mail-order catalog she went to Canada.

❧❈❧

Blue Rhapsody • 1991 • $300.00

As the first exclusive for Service Merchandise, Blue Rhapsody is hard to find. Service Merchandise is not known for packing their dolls gently; consequently, like Blossom Beautiful, many boxes are damaged. Collectors whose main interest is not perfect boxes, tend to be more forgiving of imperfections and are lucky to have either of these two dolls.

❧❈❧

Satin Nights • 1992 • $65.00

It's easy to see why Satin Nights is so popular. Her eye make-up is simple and elegant, the colors are rich, and the whole effect is enhanced by just the right amount of rouge. There are few outfits available for Barbie in black and white, adding to her popularity. There are two versions of this doll: one has all white plastic earrings as you see here, the other has silver and white earrings. There is a difference in the necklaces.

Sparkling Splendor • 1993 • $35.00

Sparkling Splendor has the silkiest long blonde hair. It's easy to comb. Her lips look red in this photo, but they look orange on my doll. Barbie doll's gown is true red and her shoes are rose pink. The artwork on the box is stunning. We are seeing increased attention to design and art in packaging. Nice touch!

Blossom Beauty • 1991 • $55.00

Shopko/Venture only had two dolls. These were the only two customized dolls wearing formal dresses with printed flowers. The print is a bit larger than scale for Barbie. The jewel tone colors are a dramatic combination.

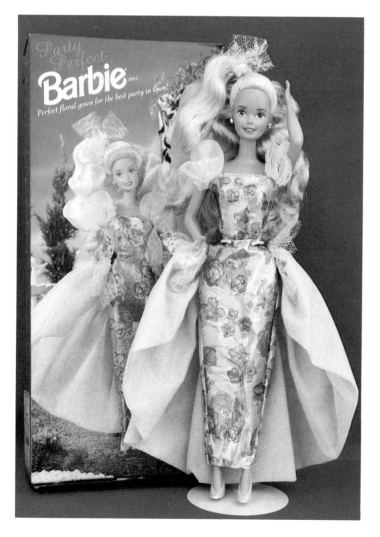

Party Perfect • 1992 • $45.00

Party Perfect Barbie doll's floral gown has a metallic sheen. She's dressed for a party, always ready for fun.

Singapore Girl I • 1991 • $125.00

This unique doll is extremely hard to acquire. She is not well known. If you had the opportunity to fly on Singapore Airlines, you could buy her in flight. She came in a narrow brown box, very basic. The doll is wearing the official Singapore Airline stewardess uniform. Will this doll escalate to the value that the Braniff Airline doll did? Time will tell.

Singapore Girl II • 1991 • $125.00

I just recently discovered that there is this second version of Singapore Girl. I had seen her at a show, and mentally noted that her make-up was considerably better than my doll's and that her hair was fuller. I looked at her for the longest time and didn't realize she was in a different box. Unfortunately, I left her sitting there. I was lucky to find her again at the very next show. The boxes were not released simultaneously, yet they carry the same pattern date.

≈ ✿ ৩

Singapore Girl I and II

≈ ✿ ৩

Sterling Wishes • 1991 • $150.00

Spiegel joined Mattel in selecting better dolls for their exclusive. The fabric of choice for their first doll, Sterling Wishes, is velvet and silver lamé, an elegant combination. The richness of the fabric and quality of construction was higher than her opening price would indicate. She is extremely popular with the advanced collector. But wait until you see what came next...

Regal Reflections • 1992 • $350.00

Regal Reflections, the second for Spiegel, is an example of the exception to the rule; that being the first in the series commands the money. This Barbie is not easy to find; her production level seems to be considerably lower. Her outfit is tasteful and elaborate and shows a Spanish influence.

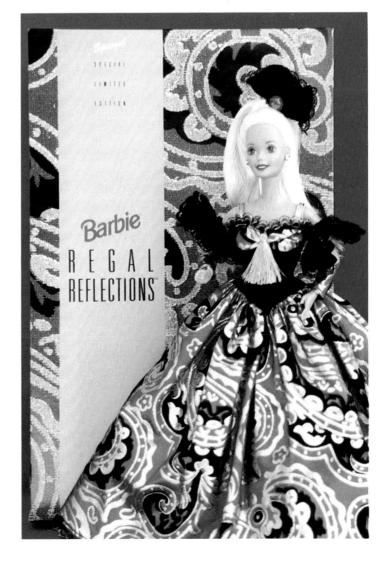

Royal Invitation • 1993 • $125.00

It's hard to say whether this, the third Spiegel doll was less well received or whether her production level was increased over demand. She is easy to find and her value has not jumped tremendously. Royal Invitation's gown, although elaborately constructed, was not quite as high grade as her two predecessors'. The artwork on her box is terrific and is a treasure in itself.

Pretty Hearts • 1991 • $25.00

A number of different grocery store chains across the country get to share in these specials. Not all grocery stores are represented everywhere. Pretty Hearts was the first in a long-running series of cute, inexpensive supermarket Barbie doll's. The first five all have straight arms. This doll and dress are identical to the doll used for the Friendship Barbie, which commemorated the tearing down of the Berlin Wall. Both were a redesign of Pretty Hearts Barbie, a regular line doll from the 1980's.

Sweet Spring • 1991 • $25.00

Sweet Spring was released around Easter and probably wound up in many a little girl's Easter baskets. Her little frock, straw hat, and matching straw bag are perfect for a spring day.

Trailblazin' • 1991 • $25.00

Western dolls continue to sell well long after production ceases. Trailblazin' Barbie is a good example. She's popular because she's cute, has a beautiful face, western attire, and is still reasonably priced.

Party Premiere • 1992 • $25.00

Party Premiere is the only exclusive with raspberry colored lips to match her raspberry party dress. The lamé bodice adds to her value and gives a touch of elegance to a low budget doll.

Red Romance • 1992 • $25.00

Pretty Hearts Barbie was released at Valentine's in February. She was such a success, and such a great gift idea (I'd rather get a Barbie than roses) that they repeated the concept with Red Romance. Could the stars in her eyes indicate true love?

≈ ⚬⚬⚬ ⚬

Spring Bouquet • 1992 • $25.00

Easter and spring came together with Spring Bouquet Barbie. Pastel colors traditionally open the fashion season. It's only natural that this Barbie be dressed in an airy pastel day dress.

≈ ⚬⚬⚬ ⚬

Back to School • 1992 • $25.00

By the beginning of September Back to School Barbie was released. She was appropriately timed and designed to offer inspiration for children everywhere to get motivated to return to classes.

Holiday Hostess • 1992 • $45.00

Holiday Hostess was the first Barbie in the supermarket circuit to reflect the holiday season. Dressed as Santa's helper, she was instantly a favorite for collectors. Many collectors who don't buy exclusives bought her to add to their holiday doll series. I predict her value will escalate as supply diminishes.

Easter Fun • 1993 • $35.00

This fabric printed specially for Barbie, truly made for Easter Fun. She comes with instructions for an Easter egg hunt game and decorations for the eggs. These added accessories make it a bonus buy. Many of the supermarkets across the country did not stock the doll, so she is a bit harder to find in some parts of the country.

B mine • 1993 • $35.00

For three years running, there were three great Valentine dolls. B mine Barbie, appropriately named, wears a specially designed fabric with cordial candy hearts. She has red-hot heart earrings that are not edible, nor are the hearts on her dress. Both Easter Fun Barbie and B mine Barbie were available as regular line dolls in some parts of Europe.

Gold & Lace • 1989 • $40.00

Woolworth's has the most single dolls designed specifically for them, but Target is a close second. It all started with Gold & Lace Barbie. She was promoted as the center of attention at the party, and with such a perky little dress, she must have been.

Party Pretty • 1990 • $35.00

Party Pretty Barbie has been found NRFB in three different versions. One is in a textured black dress trimmed with white lace and matching jacket with snail trail, an iridescent fabrication. The second is a black nylon dress trimmed with chantilly lace and jacket to match. The third is a lace textured dress trimmed with chantilly lace; Barbie doll's jacket has snail trail. Could there be a fourth version with snail trail trimmed skirt and chantilly jacket, the reverse of number three?

Golden Evening • 1991 • $40.00

I know you thought I was going to say that Pretty In Plaid was my favorite Target doll, but no, Golden Evening Barbie is. She consistently has the nicest make-up of any of the inexpensive exclusives. Her night-on-the-town attire is a higher grade than most dolls' outfits in this category. She displays well with the best of them.

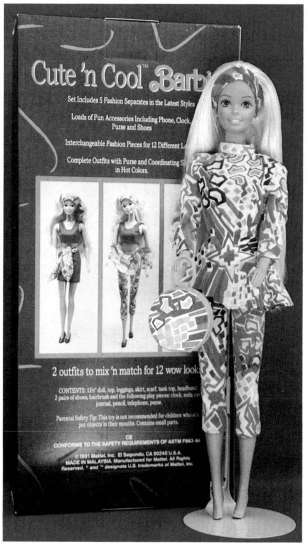

Cute 'n Cool • 1991 • $25.00

Cute 'n Cool Barbie was distrib-
uted by the Dayton Hudson Cor-
poration, which owns Target. The
colors used in Barbie doll's box
are the ones used in Dayton Hudson's logo. Cute 'n Cool comes
with extra pieces that create
twelve different ensembles. She
has purple flats and orange
pumps. Barbie looks better out of
the box than in it. The pale colored liner and sienna box detracts
from the beauty of this doll.

Wild Style • 1992 • $25.00

Wild Style Barbie, fifth for Target, is a border-line biker. She isn't quite here or there with her 1950's collar jacket, 1960's satin cap, and printed leggings that aren't quite Emilio Pucci. Maybe this mixture is good; it leaves more to the imagination.

Dazzlin' Date • 1992 • $25.00

Target has ten dolls, not including the variations. Of the ten, Dazzlin' Date Barbie is the fourth party-dressed doll. Target has yet to offer its customers a doll wearing a floor length dress.

Pretty In Plaid • 1992 • $25.00

When Mattel went looking for fabric for this doll, I can't say I know where they went to get it. In case you've lost count, this is number seven.

Bathtime Fun Skipper • 1992 • $25.00

The only non-Barbie exclusive for Target was this Bathtime Fun Skipper. Mattel had made Bathtime Barbie for the mass market and it was sold in toy stores everywhere. These bath toys encourage children to submerge their dolls in water. Mothers and children need to be advised that not all Barbie doll's are compatible with water. This is definitely not recommended play for your Bob Mackie dolls.

Baseball Barbie • 1993 • $25.00

Baseball Barbie was part of a sports theme used with other mass marketed dolls. In 1993, there was one other sports related exclusive (see next page). Other athletically inclined dolls included Stacie and Todd playing soccer, Rollerblade Barbie and friends, and a very cute baseball uniform sold separately for Ken. Ken in his uniform and Baseball Barbie make a fun display.

Golf Date • 1992 • $25.00

Golf Date Barbie in her argyle sweater, popular attire for real golfers, is ready for a day on the course. Sports related activities for Barbie continues; watch for more in the future. P. S. Barbie doll's argyle sweater is the same fabric used on the European version of Benetton Shopping Teresa.

Pink Jubilee • 1987 • $85.00

Walmart celebrated its 25th year in business with a first exclusive for them, Pink Jubilee Barbie. Her outfit was created to offer ten different looks. This doesn't mean you have to have ten different dolls; it just means you have to have plenty of playtime to keep changing Barbie doll's outfits. This doll was also available in Canada as Party Pink.

Frills & Fantasy • 1988 • $65.00

Frills & Fantasy is the only exclusive with little rosette earrings and a matching necklace.

Lavender Looks • 1989 • $55.00

Walmart's third doll is Lavender Looks Barbie. As you can see by the photo her skirt becomes an evening wrap. Clever! Walmart consistently selects good looking dolls for their chain.

Dream Fantasy • 1990 • $45.00

It's hard to pick a favorite Walmart doll. For a minute I selected Dream Fantasy, then I changed my mind and picked Ballroom Beauty, then decided on Frills & Fantasy...oh, I can't make up my mind. Can you?

Ballroom Beauty • 1991 • $45.00

If you were going to attend a ball, what would you wear? Ballroom Beauty Barbie doll's ensemble could be worn six different ways.

Anniversary Star • 1992 • $40.00

1992 marked Walmart's 30th year in business, so Mattel gave Barbie a special sash and silver hang tag to commemorate the celebration. The supply on Anniversary Star was good but she did not stay on the shelves long, at least not in my area. This doll and ensemble were also found in Germany at Vedes stores wearing the Vedes logo.

Superstar Barbie • 1993 • $35.00

Back in 1976, Mattel released a regular line doll called Superstar Barbie of which there were many versions over a number of years. Superstar had a very long production life and each was a success. Then in 1993, Walmart selected this Superstar doll complete with a miniature Barbie-like Oscar similar to the one found in the early versions. This doll was also available in some parts of Europe as a regular line doll.

Superstar Barbie • 1993 • $35.00

Walmart also offered Superstar Barbie in an ethnic model. She came with all the accessories as the white version. Many consider her Hispanic in spite of her Cristie face mold.

Toothfairy • 1993 • $25.00

The ninth Barbie for Walmart is a new concept, Toothfairy Barbie. She comes with a metallic drawstring bag for a child to put her lost tooth in and put under her pillow. This way her tooth won't get lost while she is waiting for the fairy to bring money so she can buy another Barbie.

❧ ❀ ❧

Country Star Barbie • $25.00

We love these western style outfits. Barbie doll's ruffled frock is made from the identical fabric as Janet Goldblatt's Classique fashion, Flower Shower, which is sold in specialty stores only.

❧ ❀ ❧

Country Star Teresa • $25.00

Country Star Teresa is our first non-Barbie for Walmart. She's cute as a button, right down to her boots! There is a third verson, black Country Western Star Barbie.

Party Sensation • 1990 • $55.00

1990 was the first year Mattel solicited
wholesale clubs across the country to
participate in the customized program.
Party Sensation Barbie started a chain
reaction. Collector interest in obtaining
harder-to-find dolls increased substan-
tially just as wholesale clubs started
handling exclusives. Mattel had extras
of this gorgeous doll and shared it with
specialty doll shops. Many of the wholesale clubs share Barbie dolls so I have
decided to put them all in one category
to avoid duplication.

Jewel Jubilee • 1991 • $85.00

I don't remember seeing Jewel Jubilee very long on the shelves. She does turn up at shows enough to keep her price stable. I like the way she blended in with my Summit dolls, so that's where I have her displayed. She was originally found at Sam's and Pace.

Royal Romance • 1992 • $55.00

Royal Romance has a beautiful and yet simple face paint. Mattel cut corners by not cutting her hem straight. Many of the dolls have jagged, raw hemlines, but nothing that a sharp pair of scissors won't shape up. She was offered at Price Club.

Very Violet • 1992 • $55.00

It's always fun to note the difference between what's on the box and the final product. Bob Gardner tells me that this is because the boxes and designs of the boxes are made well in advance of the doll and that the dolls used on the box are prototypes or samples. If you look hard at the photo you will see that Barbie doll's skirt has a paisley pattern, not a floral one and that the roses on the bodice have been raised. This doll was also available in 1993 through Mattel France, mail order only. In the U.S. you could have found her at Pace.

Fantastica • 1992 •$55.00

Here's our first ethnically dressed exclusive. Many Barbie collectors who don't acquire exclusives bought her, as did I, to display with the International/Dolls of the World series. Mattel chose Rollerblade Theresa's face mold, one of my favorite molds. Fantastica would have been found at either Pace or Sam's.

Peach Blossom • 1992 • $55.00

Peach Blossom makes a delightful display with Peach Pretty and Peaches 'n Cream. As you can see in the close-up, Mattel blended Barbie doll's face and make-up really well with a soft peachy plastic. The combination softens the doll and enhances the gown. Peach Blossom was exclusive to Sam's.

~ ❦ ~

Cinderella Gift Set • 1992 • $125.00

This is one of the most unusual packagings to date. It more resembles a store display prop than a gift set. This Cinderella must have been very scarce, as very few know of her existence. It was made from regular line Disney Classics. (See Jasmine page 135.)

~ ❦ ~

Sun Sensation • 1992 • $65.00

This Sun Sensation doll was a regular line beach doll and by herself sold for under $10.00. In this gift set version you get a swimming pool for Barbie that sprays water when you push the pump.

Rollerblade Gift Set • 1992 • $65.00

Arco, a Mattel company, made gift sets for the wholesale clubs. Accessories, fashions, and contents varied greatly. This hot dog stand would be right at home on Venice Beach, California. In previous years the stand was sold separately at toy stores.

Sparkle Eye Gift Set • 1992 • $65.00

Sparkle Eye Barbie and Ken were released as regular line dolls, then Barbie was packaged here with her own dressing room and fashion set.

100 Piece Gift Set • 1992 • $55.00

There were two versions of this gift set also. Each had a different doll dressed in different outfits.

Holiday Gown Collection I • 1992 • $75.00

I intended to just concentrate on the dolls, but this gift set of holiday ensembles for Barbie, made by Arco, is just too important to leave out. Holiday doll collectors did not hesitate to add this to their displays.

Winter Royal • 1993 • $65.00

Fur trimmed gowns are very popular with collectors. The 1989 Holiday Barbie, Winter Fantasy, Winter Princess, and JC Penney's Enchanted Evening with their faux fur are amongst the most popular in this price range. Winter Royal was another wholesale club doll that Mattel shared with specialty doll shops.

A glorious vision of beauty graces the wintry landscape. In her regal, elegant gown she stands poised beside her shimmering sleigh, ready to be whisked away to a royal extravaganza. She is Winter Royale Barbie, a tribute to the majestic splendor of winter.

Festiva • 1993 • $55.00

Festiva, our second ethnic exclusive, following Fantastica, was created for a wholesale club. It is very unclear what happened, no one's talking at Mattel. Only a few hit the market on schedule. Prices skyrocketed immediately. Collectors were screaming for her. She was to have been released in the fall of 1993. Then in 1994, Mattel told the specialty shops that they could order Festiva. We did, and then we waited and waited and waited. Finally, they released her. Prices came down and are now back up. For those who paid an early high price, just remember that no one knew what was happening with Festiva and it was better to have one than not at all.

Island Fun • 1993 • $35.00

Island Fun Barbie & Ken gift set was very reasonably priced. There weren't many of these found and they disappeared from the shelves very quickly. There aren't that many two-doll gift sets available. Lucky is the collector who has them.

Every bride is a princess on her wedding day. I want my wedding to be just how I've always dreamed it would be. One day I'll marry Ken. We'll get married in the most beautiful garden imaginable! All of our friends will be there. And, I want roses everywhere, even tiny pink ones on my dress! It'll be so romantic. Oh well, for now it's just a dream!

Wedding Fantasy • 1993 • $95.00

Again, another two-doll gift set. Very rare! Wedding themes are always popular. Mattel created a lovely doll. If you don't have it and you see it, buy it!

Hollywood Hair Gift Set • 1993 • $35.00

This gift set was produced in great quantity. Many collectors may have resisted it because so many bought the single regular line version.

Western Stompin' Gift Set • 1993 • $45.00

The same applies to Western Stompin' Gift Set as did with Hollywood Hair. However, Western dolls are more popular. Barbie comes with an extra outfit which is exclusive to this set and two stamp pads with her boots as stamps.

Paint 'n Dazzle Gift Set • 1993 • $35.00

This gift set offered a lot of play time for an older child or younger girl with mom's help. It came with many extras that the single, regular line Barbie didn't have. Again, the extra outfit can only be gotten by purchasing this gift set.

Secret Heart Gift Set • 1993 • $55.00

Ice cubes applied to the fabric on Secret Heart Barbie doll's gown cause hearts to appear. Mattel made a special carriage for Barbie and Ken that was available only in Europe and in specialty shops in the U. S. Ken's outfit is exclusive to this two-doll gift set. Note that Ken's hair in this gift set is blond, even though the photo on the box shows a brunet. Ken's hair is brown in the regular line version.

Jasmine Gift Set • 1993 • $100.00

What a nice surprise to have a repeat packaging like the one we saw in 1992 with Cinderella. Again, very rare. Disney collectors as well as Barbie collectors will want this gift set.

Show White & Seven Dwarf Gift Set • 1993 • $150.00

There were many Snow White packages available: Snow White alone, with stackable dwarfs, or this, the rarest combination of all, Snow White and all seven dwarfs. The initial outlay seemed like a lot of money but considering all you got in this one box, combined with its rarity, you really have a treasure.

Beach Fun Barbie & Ken • 1993 • $35.00

This Barbie and Ken gift set is a sister
piece to Island Fun. The concept is the
same and at first glance you might think
you already have it. Look again.

Dressing Fun Gift Set • 1993 • $55.00

This gift set was also referred to as "Lots of Fashions." If you like dressing and undressing your dolls, this should fill your day. Note the two versions.

Top: box, lavender dress • Bottom: box, pink dress

Holiday Gown Collection II • 1993 • $55.00

Once again Arco's Holiday gowns were available in a gift pak. There are few Barbie collectors who don't have the holiday dolls, so why not have the Holiday gowns? Do you recognize any of the dolls modeling these dresses? Nope, me either.

Party Pink • 1989 • $35.00

Party Pink, for Winn Dixie, was in my opinion the forerunner to what developed into the Supermarket Special category that we are familiar with today. Winn Dixie only had three dolls. The first two had straight arms. She was also available in Europe with a different hair style and different name.

Contents: Doll, party dress, panties, shoes, hairbrush

Pink Sensation • 1990 • $30.00

Sometimes you get a doll and her hair is unmanageable, and you wonder if they are all like that, or if you are the only lucky one. A similar version was released in Europe with another name.

Southern Beauty • 1991 • $30.00

Most of the inexpensive dolls found in chain stores have straight arms. But here Southern Beauty Barbie has bent arms. Her dress is a higher grade than her predecessors' gowns.

≈ ✼ ≈

Special Expressions • 1989 • $35.00

I had not concentrated on the Woolworth dolls for my own collection. So when it came time to do this book, I went scrambling for these dolls. They seemed to be everywhere and cheap. They were cheap until I added in the cost of my phone bill to get them. Unfortunately, I was not able to secure them all. 1989 was Woolworth's first year. There were two dolls, one white, one black; wearing a cute white nylon dress with lace trim.

≈ ✼ ≈

Special Expressions • 1989 • $35.00

This would be a good time to remind you that these dolls are listed by patent date on the box, not year released. When I was ordering these dolls from other shopkeepers I couldn't understand how I kept ending up with the same doll, over and over again. The patent date is not necessarily the date it was released.

Special Expressions • 1990 • $30.00

Again, Woolworth offered just two dolls, white and black. Barbie doll's little one shoulder chiffon dress is fun for summer.

Special Expression • 1990 • $30.00

Dressed the same as the white version, Barbie is ready to party.

Special Expressions •1991 • $25.00

For the third year running there were just two dolls. Another chiffon dress, this one in aqua, has a lace bodice.

Special Expressions • 1991 • $35.00

The liners that accompanied these two 1991 dolls were different colors.

Special Expressions • 1992 • $25.00

There were three dolls this year. The salmon colored dress reminds us of Winn Dixie. However, when put side by side the colors are very different. She was released in 1992.

Special Expressions • 1992 • $35.00

The Hispanic dolls, when first released were reported as being more scarce than the black dolls. Collectors love this face mold. She was the first Woolworth Hispanic.

Special Expressions • 1992 • N/A

If you collect the Woolworth dolls and you don't have have this one, I would recommend that you don't hesitate to buy her. (Photo of box courtesy of Judy Schizas.)

Sweet Lavender • 1992 • $40.00

This was the first formally dressed Barbie for Woolworth. She was only produced in a white and black version. Sweet Lavender's bodice is the same fabric as used on FAO Schwarz's Rockettes (see page 38). The black dolls were produced in considerably less numbers. This Sweet Lavender Barbie is super in this gown. The colors are particularly good with her eye shadow.

∾ �֍ ∾

Special Expressions • 1993 • $25.00

This Special Expressions Barbie was the first and only to wear a cotton printed dress. The colors are particularly good with her face paint. She was released in 1993.

∾ ✷ ∾

Special Expressions • 1993 • $25.00

Woolworth continued with three Special Expressions. This Hispanic version was released in 1993.

Special Expressions • 1993 • N/A

This doll was nearly impossible for me to find for this book. She was released into the marketplace in 1993.

About the Author

Margo Rana remembers clearly Christmas 1959 when she got her first Barbie. She remembers visiting her cousins in Orlando, who had gotten their first Barbie dolls for their birthdays. Margo wanted one too. It was sad she had to wait until Christmas to get one, but when she did, she was the happiest little girl. From that day on Barbie went everywhere with her, that is until she was thirteen and her friends weren't interested in dolls anymore even though Margo wanted to continue to play.

Then in 1980, the discovery of black and Hispanic Barbie on the shelf of a local store, sent Margo into a tizzy. Before she knew it her interest had rekindled, the collection grew, and new interests developed. Taking pictures and writing articles for various publications was another aspect of the hobby of Barbie, which eventually evolved into this book.

Margo keeps herself too busy with her doll shop in Santa Barbara, selling at doll shows, and keeping a house, four cats, and a dog.

Margo Rana, third from left.

Books on Antiques and Collectibles

This is only a partial listing of the books on antiques that are available from Collector Books. All books are well illustrated and contain current values. Most of the following books are available from your local book seller, antique dealer, or public library. If you are unable to locate certain titles in your area, you may order by mail from COLLECTOR BOOKS, P.O. Box 3009, Paducah, KY 42002-3009. Customers with Visa or MasterCard may phone in orders from 8:00–4:00 CST, Monday–Friday, Toll Free 1-800-626-5420. Add $2.00 for postage for the first book ordered and $0.30 for each additional book. Include item number, title, and price when ordering. Allow 14 to 21 days for delivery.

BOOKS ON GLASS AND POTTERY

1810	American Art Glass, Shuman	$29.95
1312	Blue & White Stoneware, McNerney	$9.95
1959	Blue Willow, 2nd Ed., Gaston	$14.95
3719	Coll. Glassware from the 40's, 50's, 60's, 2nd Ed., Florence	$19.95
3816	Collectible Vernon Kilns, Nelson	$24.95
3311	Collecting Yellow Ware – Id. & Value Gd., McAllister	$16.95
1373	Collector's Ency. of American Dinnerware, Cunningham	$24.95
3815	Coll. Ency. of Blue Ridge Dinnerware, Newbound	$19.95
2272	Collector's Ency. of California Pottery, Chipman	$24.95
3811	Collector's Ency. of Colorado Pottery, Carlton	$24.95
3312	Collector's Ency. of Children's Dishes, Whitmyer	$19.95
2133	Collector's Ency. of Cookie Jars, Roerig	$24.95
3723	Coll. Ency. of Cookie Jars-Volume II, Roerig	$24.95
3724	Collector's Ency. of Depression Glass, 11th Ed., Florence	$19.95
2209	Collector's Ency. of Fiesta, 7th Ed., Huxford	$19.95
1439	Collector's Ency. of Flow Blue China, Gaston	$19.95
3812	Coll. Ency. of Flow Blue China, 2nd Ed., Gaston	$24.95
3813	Collector's Ency. of Hall China, 2nd Ed., Whitmyer	$24.95
2334	Collector's Ency. of Majolica Pottery, Katz-Marks	$19.95
1358	Collector's Ency. of McCoy Pottery, Huxford	$19.95
3313	Collector's Ency. of Niloak, Gifford	$19.95
3837	Collector's Ency. of Nippon Porcelain I, Van Patten	$24.95
2089	Collector's Ency. of Nippon Porcelain II, Van Patten	$24.95
1665	Collector's Ency. of Nippon Porcelain III, Van Patten	$24.95
1447	Collector's Ency. of Noritake, 1st Series, Van Patten	$19.95
1034	Collector's Ency. of Roseville Pottery, Huxford	$19.95
1035	Collector's Ency. of Roseville Pottery, 2nd Ed., Huxford	$19.95
3314	Collector's Ency. of Van Briggle Art Pottery, Sasicki	$24.95
3433	Collector's Guide To Harker Pottery - U.S.A., Colbert	$17.95
2339	Collector's Guide to Shawnee Pottery, Vanderbilt	$19.95
1425	Cookie Jars, Westfall	$9.95
3440	Cookie Jars, Book II, Westfall	$19.95
2275	Czechoslovakian Glass & Collectibles, Barta	$16.95
3882	Elegant Glassware of the Depression Era, 6th Ed., Florence	$19.95
3725	Fostoria - Pressed, Blown & Hand Molded Shapes, Kerr	$24.95
3883	Fostoria Stemware - The Crystal for America, Long	$24.95
3886	Kitchen Glassware of the Depression Years, 5th Ed., Florence	$19.95
3889	Pocket Guide to Depression Glass, 9th Ed., Florence	$9.95
3825	Puritan Pottery, Morris	$24.95
1670	Red Wing Collectibles, DePasquale	$9.95
1440	Red Wing Stoneware, DePasquale	$9.95
1958	So. Potteries Blue Ridge Dinnerware, 3rd Ed., Newbound	$14.95
3739	Standard Carnival Glass, 4th Ed., Edwards	$24.95
3327	Watt Pottery – Identification & Value Guide, Morris	$19.95
2224	World of Salt Shakers, 2nd Ed., Lechner	$24.95

BOOKS ON DOLLS & TOYS

2079	Barbie Fashion, Vol. 1, 1959-1967, Eames	$24.95
3310	Black Dolls – 1820 - 1991 – Id. & Value Guide, Perkins	$17.95
3810	Chatty Cathy Dolls, Lewis	$15.95
1529	Collector's Ency. of Barbie Dolls, DeWein	$19.95
2338	Collector's Ency. of Disneyana, Longest & Stern	$24.95
3727	Coll. Guide to Ideal Dolls, Izen	$18.95
3822	Madame Alexander Price Guide #19, Smith	$9.95
3732	Matchbox Toys, 1948 to 1993, Johnson	$18.95

3733	Modern Collector's Dolls, 6th series, Smith	$24.95
1540	Modern Toys, 1930 - 1980, Baker	$19.95
3824	Patricia Smith's Doll Values – Antique to Modern, 10th ed.	$12.95
3826	Story of Barbie, Westenhouser, No Values	$19.95
2028	Toys, Antique & Collectible, Longest	$14.95
1808	Wonder of Barbie, Manos	$9.95
1430	World of Barbie Dolls, Manos	$9.95

OTHER COLLECTIBLES

1457	American Oak Furniture, McNerney	$9.95
3716	American Oak Furniture, Book II, McNerney	$12.95
2333	Antique & Collectible Marbles, 3rd Ed., Grist	$9.95
1748	Antique Purses, Holiner	$19.95
1426	Arrowheads & Projectile Points, Hothem	$7.95
1278	Art Nouveau & Art Deco Jewelry, Baker	$9.95
1714	Black Collectibles, Gibbs	$19.95
1128	Bottle Pricing Guide, 3rd Ed., Cleveland	$7.95
3717	Christmas Collectibles, 2nd Ed., Whitmyer	$24.95
1752	Christmas Ornaments, Johnston	$19.95
3718	Collectible Aluminum, Grist	$16.95
2132	Collector's Ency. of American Furniture, Vol. I, Swedberg	$24.95
2271	Collector's Ency. of American Furniture, Vol. II, Swedberg	$24.95
3720	Coll. Ency. of American Furniture, Vol III, Swedberg	$24.95
3722	Coll. Ency. of Compacts, Carryalls & Face Powder Boxes, Mueller	$24.95
2018	Collector's Ency. of Granite Ware, Greguire	$24.95
3430	Coll. Ency. of Granite Ware, Book 2, Greguire	$24.95
1441	Collector's Guide to Post Cards, Wood	$9.95
2276	Decoys, Kangas	$24.95
1629	Doorstops – Id. & Values, Bertoia	$9.95
1716	Fifty Years of Fashion Jewelry, Baker	$19.95
3817	Flea Market Trader, 9th Ed., Huxford	$12.95
3731	Florence's Standard Baseball Card Price Gd., 6th Ed.	$9.95
3819	General Store Collectibles, Wilson	$24.95
3436	Grist's Big Book of Marbles, Everett Grist	$19.95
2278	Grist's Machine Made & Contemporary Marbles	$9.95
1424	Hatpins & Hatpin Holders, Baker	$9.95
3884	Huxford's Collectible Advertising – Id. & Value Gd., 2nd Ed	$24.95
3820	Huxford's Old Book Value Guide, 6th Ed.	$19.95
3821	Huxford's Paperback Value Guide	$19.95
1181	100 Years of Collectible Jewelry, Baker	$9.95
2216	Kitchen Antiques – 1790 - 1940, McNerney	$14.95
3887	Modern Guns – Id. & Val. Gd., 10th Ed., Quertermous	$12.95
3734	Pocket Guide to Handguns, Quertermous	$9.95
3735	Pocket Guide to Rifles, Quertermous	$9.95
3736	Pocket Guide to Shotguns, Quertermous	$9.95
2026	Railroad Collectibles, 4th Ed., Baker	$14.95
1632	Salt & Pepper Shakers, Guarnaccia	$9.95
1888	Salt & Pepper Shakers II, Guarnaccia	$14.95
2220	Salt & Pepper Shakers III, Guarnaccia	$14.95
3443	Salt & Pepper Shakers IV, Guarnaccia	$18.95
3890	Schroeder's Antiques Price Guide, 13th Ed.	$12.95
2096	Silverplated Flatware, 4th Ed., Hagan	$14.95
2348	20th Century Fashionable Plastic Jewelry, Baker	$19.95
3828	Value Guide to Advertising Memorabilia, Summers	$18.95
3830	Vintage Vanity Bags & Purses, Gerson	$24.95

Schroeder's
ANTIQUES
Price Guide

. . . is the #1 best-selling antiques & collectibles value guide on the market today, and here's why . . .

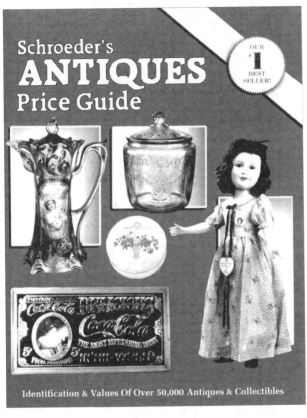

Schroeder's
ANTIQUES
Price Guide

OUR #1 BEST SELLER!

Identification & Values Of Over 50,000 Antiques & Collectibles

8½ x 11, 608 Pages, $14.95

• *More than 300 advisors, well-known dealers, and top-notch collectors work together with our editors to bring you accurate information regarding pricing and identification.*

• *More than 45,000 items in almost 500 categories are listed along with hundreds of sharp original photos that illustrate not only the rare and unusual, but the common, popular collectibles as well.*

• *Each large close-up shot shows important details clearly. Every subject is represented with histories and background information, a feature not found in any of our competitors' publications.*

• *Our editors keep abreast of newly developing trends, often adding several new categories a year as the need arises.*

If it merits the interest of today's collector, you'll find it in *Schroeder's*. And you can feel confident that the information we publish is up to date and accurate. Our advisors thoroughly check each category to spot inconsistencies, listings that may not be entirely reflective of market dealings, and lines too vague to be of merit. Only the best of the lot remains for publication.

Without doubt, you'll find
SCHROEDER'S ANTIQUES PRICE GUIDE
the only one to buy for
reliable information and values.

COLLECTOR BOOKS
A Division of Schroeder Publishing Co., Inc.